What's It WORTH?

RACHEL FIRST

Consulting Editor, Diane Craig, M.A./Reading Specialist

Sandcastle

An Imprint of Abdo Publishing
abdopublishing.com

abdopublishing.com

Published by Abdo Publishing, a division of ABDO, PO Box 398166, Minneapolis, Minnesota 55439. Copyright © 2016 by Abdo Consulting Group, Inc. International copyrights reserved in all countries. No part of this book may be reproduced in any form without written permission from the publisher. SandCastle™ is a trademark and logo of Abdo Publishing.

Printed in the United States of America, North Mankato, Minnesota

102015
012016

THIS BOOK CONTAINS
RECYCLED MATERIALS

Editor: Liz Salzmann
Content Developer: Nancy Tuminelly
Cover and Interior Design and Production: Mighty Media, Inc.
Photo Credits: Shutterstock, Wikimedia Commons

Library of Congress Cataloging-in-Publication Data

First, Rachel, author.
 What's it worth? : fun with coins & bills / Rachel First ; consulting editor, Diane Craig, M.A./ reading specialist.
    pages cm. -- (Math beginnings)
 ISBN 978-1-62403-937-9
 1. Money--Juvenile literature. I. Title. II. Title: What is it worth?
 HG221.5.F574 2016
 332.4--dc23
                    2015020615

SandCastle™ Level: Transitional

SandCastle™ books are created by a team of professional educators, reading specialists, and content developers around five essential components—phonemic awareness, phonics, vocabulary, text comprehension, and fluency—to assist young readers as they develop reading skills and strategies and increase their general knowledge. All books are written, reviewed, and leveled for guided reading, early reading intervention, and Accelerated Reader™ programs for use in shared, guided, and independent reading and writing activities to support a balanced approach to literacy instruction. The SandCastle™ series has four levels that correspond to early literacy development. The levels are provided to help teachers and parents select appropriate books for young readers.

EMERGING · BEGINNING · **TRANSITIONAL** · FLUENT

Contents

What Do You BUY?

We use money every day.

Money lets us buy things.
What do you buy?

Money **includes** coins and bills. They are all **worth** different amounts.

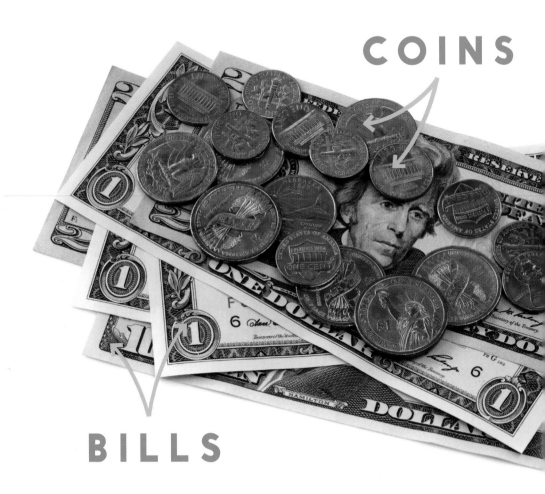

COINS

BILLS

Try It!

Search for money at home. Ask an adult to help. Sort what you find. Put the coins in one pile. Put the bills in another pile.

COINS

penny = 1 cent

nickel = 5 cents

dime = 10 cents

quarter = 25 cents

Coins are made of **metal**. They are **worth** cents. A penny is worth 1 cent. It is the lowest amount.

half-dollar = 50 cents   dollar coin = 100 cents

BILLS

one-dollar bill =
1 dollar

five-dollar bill =
5 dollars

ten-dollar bill =
10 dollars

Bills are made of paper.
They are **worth** dollars. The
smallest bill is worth 1 dollar.

twenty-dollar bill =
20 dollars

fifty-dollar bill =
50 dollars

one hundred-dollar bill =
100 dollars

DOLLARS and CENTS

100 pennies = 1 dollar

20 nickels = 1 dollar

10 dimes = 1 dollar

Cents add up to dollars. There
are 100 cents in 1 dollar. How
many of each coin would that be?

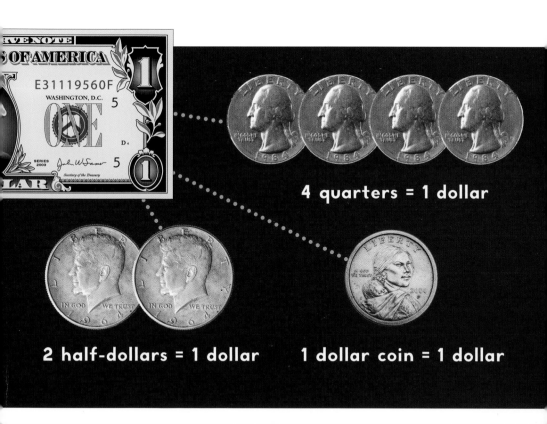

4 quarters = 1 dollar

2 half-dollars = 1 dollar

1 dollar coin = 1 dollar

Smaller bills can be used together.
They add up to larger amounts.

 =

 =

You can add coins and bills together too. It's Mya's birthday. Her grandpa gave her some birthday money.

He gave her bills and coins. How much does she have?

Try It!

Write down the amount of each coin and bill. How many dollars are there? How many cents?

PRICES

A price tells how much something costs. The price can be a cent amount. It uses a cent sign.

A price can be a dollar
amount. It uses a dollar sign.

A price can have dollars and cents. It uses a **decimal point**. The dollars are on the left. The decimal point is in the middle. The cents are on the right.

PRACTICE

Look at the pictures on the right.
How much money is in each
group? Think about it.
Then follow
the lines
with your
finger.
Were you
right?

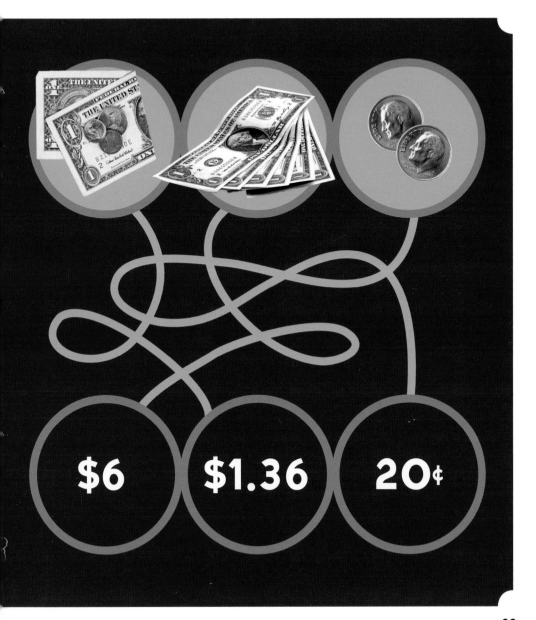

$6 $1.36   20¢

Glossary

DECIMAL POINT — a dot in a price that separates the dollars and cents.

INCLUDE — to have as part of a whole.

METAL — a hard, shiny material that can be made into different shapes.

WORTH — equal in value to.